The Podcast Producer's Guide to Managing Your Podcast

A Guide to Building Effective Workflows for a Smooth, Streamlined Podcast Product

KOPF CONSULTING

The Podcast Producer's Guide to Managing Your Podcast
A Guide to Building Effective Workflows for a Smooth, Streamlined Podcast Product

First Edition

ISBN: 979-8-2956-3207-5

This book is intended for informational and educational purposes only. While the author has made every effort to ensure the accuracy of the information provided, the content reflects general practices and concepts and may not apply to every situation. The author is not responsible for errors or omissions, or for outcomes resulting from the use of this information.

References to third-party tools, platforms, or services are for illustrative purposes only and do not constitute endorsement or affiliation.

ABOUT THE COMPANY

WHO WE ARE

A contributing partner in the entrepreneur journey, Kopf Consulting has been an ever evolving entity of knowledge, tools, tips, and training for those looking to expand their business online.

MISSION

Kopf Consulting seeks to empower those who want to take the reins of their business. Through checklist, guides, trainings, and consultations, they continue to encourage business owners both small and large to grow and flourish in their niche.

VISION

Kopf Consulting's vision is to be the go-to resource for new entrepreneurs and small business owners. By providing affordable assistance, budget friendly tools, and low cost training, Kopf Consulting will continue to be the unseen force helping propel businesses forward.

Topics To be covered

01

FINDING GUESTS

Where do you find potential guests? How can you fill your podcast guest list without spamming someone's inbox?

02

SCHEDULING GUESTS

When scheduling a guest, how do you ensure you have everything you need before the interview?

03

PRODUCING A SHOW

How do you prepare for your show or your guest interview? What do you need to do before pressing record?

04

EDITING A SHOW

What equipment can you use to edit your show? Where can you find music? What can be added to a podcast episode?

TOPICS TO BE COVERED

05

PUBLISHING A SHOW

Where do you publish your show? How do you get on YouTube Music, iTunes, Amazon Music, and more?

06

PROMOTING A SHOW

How do you get people to listen to your show? Where do you promote it? How do you get your guest to promote?

07

RECOMMENDATIONS

Don't want to do it yourself? Here is who we would recommend for graphic art, show notes, and audio editing.

08

EXAMPLE WORKFLOW BOARD

Ready to set up your task management system to stay organized? Here is an example of a workflow board to get you started.

***We are not liable for any results produced by the recommendations in this guide. As for software, we cannot guarantee an individual's experience. Please hire and/or use resources at your own risk. This guide is for entertainment purposes only.

HOW THIS GUIDE WORKS

Wait? Is all of this in the exact order for my first ever podcast?

Yes and no. Depending on where you are starting, the topics are the workflow we use when we produce our clients' podcast; however, if this is your first podcast EVER - there may still be pieces missing.

- Do you have your podcast art?
- Do you have your episode art?
- Did you already create an intro episode to push out your initial feed? This is not necessary but allows you to get a jump start on your RSS submissions (an iTunes submission can take 2-4 weeks.)

If this is your very first episode, you may want to take a look at the checklist on the next page to pull together the assortment of small pieces that will be used with each episode you produce. We have added helpful recommendations to the end of this guide, including graphic designers for your show art.

To make life easier, we have also added templated emails throughout for initial podcast invites, scheduling confirmations, and live push alerts (letting your guest know when their podcast is going live so they can promote it).

MANAGE YOUR PODCAST CHECKLIST

- Create Podcast Cover Art and Episode Art for Each Episode
- Create Speaker Form for Podcast Guests to Complete Prior to Interviews
- Find Potential Guests for Upcoming Podcast
- Create a tracking system to properly track upcoming episodes and guest communications/status
- Create booking calendar for potential guests
- Create automation invite for potential guests on emailing list
- Research guest background prior to interview. Prepare with intro, details, and questions.
- Edit Show Audio/Video
- Create Show Notes
- Create Transcript (if applicable)
- Schedule and Promote Podcast

FINDING GUESTS

01

WORDS OF WISDOM

Do not spam potential podcast guests! There is nothing less appealing than receiving email after email requesting for them to be on your show. Make your first email count, provide as much information as possible about your show and make signing up to be on your podcast as easy as possible!

Whether you have decided to go solo or start right out the gate with guests, finding a guest on your show is easier than you think. While there are a lot of paid services that will search for guests for you, there are several free (or free trial) options available: MatchMaker.FM, Podcastguests.com, and a favorite amongst those in the podcast world: Radioguestlist.com

With MatchMaker.FM, you are able to create a profile for your show and put who you are seeking as a guest. You are then able to search "Find guests" by location and topic to prospect potential guests for your show. All communication takes place right on the platform so you don't have to worry about sharing personal information (phone number, email, etc) until you have both agreed it is a good fit.

Another option is the Facebook group: Podcast Guest Collaboration Community - Find a Guest, Be a Guest

Not sure what to send to a prospective guest? Grab our email template on the next page!

EMAIL TEMPLATE #1A
PROSPECTIVE GUEST, NO PRIOR INTERVIEWS

Hi [First Name],

My name is [your name] and I am the host of [Podcast name], a show where [briefly list why people listen to your show.]

I am reaching out because I believe you would be an amazing guest for our show. Our target audience is [explain your listeners] and I know your background and expertise would be invaluable to our growing listenership.

A little more about my podcast: [give a synopsis of podcast]. Would this be something of interest to you?

We just recently launched and we wanted to start out with the most captivating interviews. If you are busy, I completely understand and appreciate this brief moment of your time.

If this does interest you, interviews are normally [length of interview] and conducted via [where interview will take place]. The next step would be completing this exceptionally brief speaker form [link to speaker form] so we can provide our audience will all the necessary means to connect with you (and if you have a free offer to share or upcoming project to promote, even better!).

Once the form is completed, you will be sent directly to our scheduling calendar. This way we have everything we need before the interview! We understand your time is valuable and want to make sure we are respecting it in every way possible.

Thank you,
[Your Name]

EMAIL TEMPLATE #1B

PROSPECTIVE GUEST, LIST PREVIOUS INTERVIEWS

Hi [First Name],

My name is [your name] and I am the host of [Podcast name], a show where [briefly list why people listen to your show.]

I am reaching out because I believe you would be an amazing guest for our show. Our target audience is [explain your listeners] and I know your background and expertise would be invaluable to our growing listenership.

A little more about my podcast: [give a synopsis of podcast]. We have had the honor and privilege of interviewing such amazing names as [list 3-5 top guests]. Our guests find our podcast to be freeing, fun, and a place to have real, deep conversations that matter.

Would this be something of interest to you?

If this does interest you, interviews are normally [length of interview] and conducted via [where interview will take place]. The next step would be completing this exceptionally brief speaker form [link to speaker form] so we can provide our audience will all the necessary means to connect with you (and if you have a free offer to share or upcoming project to promote, even better!).

Once the form is completed, you will be sent directly to our scheduling calendar. This way we have everything we need before the interview! We understand your time is valuable and want to make sure we are respecting it in every way possible.

Thank you,
[Your Name]

SCHEDULE GUESTS

02

WORDS OF WISDOM

Have your guest complete the speaker form BEFORE they book an interview time on your calendar. We have found over the years if a potential guest books first, it becomes a game of tag to get their headshot, bio information, social media links, and anything else you may need for their interview.

As the show progresses, you may not have to send the overly formal email invitations to potential guests. When this happens, your email responses break down to two methods of communication: 1) the templated response you send to those who inquire about being a guest but do not have name recognition or may be new to the podcast game as well or 2) the templated response to an inquire that is a recognized name in your field (or in general) and like a fish on a line, you don't want to lose them as a "podcast catch"!

In either case, both of these emails need to filter to a specific speaker form (you will need to create two). The first template mentioned above is not redirected to your scheduling calendar and will have an application style speaker form. This allows you to review the application and determine if this person is the best fit. If they are, you can simply send an email inviting them to schedule and let them know you are looking forward to having them on the show.

The second template uses an is exceptionally short/brief speaker form and only requests the absolutely necessary information. This form IS redirected to your scheduler. You don't want to let this fish dangle on the line too long so you want to get them through the process as quickly as possible.

EMAIL TEMPLATE #2A

RESPONSE TO GENERAL INQUIRY

This template is only used for filtering unknown guests. Do not use this for someone you definitely want on the show.

Hi [First Name],

Thank you so much for reaching out to be a guest on (name of podcast)!

Please feel free to fill out our application [hyperlink to application] and I will get back with you on seeing if you are a fit for us!

[Place link again to application]

Thank you,
[First Name]

We recommend using JotForms (free), Google Forms or Wufoo (just to name a few) for your application intake. JotForm has examples of Speaker Forms so you do not have to create them from scratch. We are also happy to set this up for you using our JotForm templates! .

EMAIL TEMPLATE #2B

ACCEPTANCE TO GENERAL INQUIRY ONLY

Hi [First Name],

We would LOVE to have you on the show. Please utilize the link below to schedule an interview.

We appreciate your completing our application so we should have everything we need for the interview.

If we are missing anything, we will be sure to reach out prior to your scheduled time.

[Link to Schedule]

Looking forward to connecting
[First Name]

EMAIL TEMPLATE #2C

REJECTION TO GENERAL INQUIRY ONLY

Hi [First Name],

Thank you so much for completing our application! We are currently booking out for the remainder of the year; however, we will be sure to keep your application on file and look forward to reconnecting. If you would like for [me/us] to be a guest on your podcast for the time being, please let [me/us] know!

Thank you again,
[First Name]

We do this instead of a full-out rejection to allow last minute bookings if a guest decides to cancel. You also don't know if an unknown guest is on the verge of "blowing up" and don't want to burn a bridge that may benefit you in the future.

EMAIL TEMPLATE #3
RESPONSE TO DESIRED PODCAST GUEST

Hi [First Name],

We would LOVE to have you on the show. Please utilize the link below to schedule an interview and we just need you to complete a quick speaker form (Super short!) so we can share all of your information with our audience.

Form: [link to form OR link to calendar that has a required form attached to it - see below]
Schedule Interview: [if using a stand-alone speaker form and not redirecting, add calendar link here]

Thank you,
[First Name]

For desired bookings, you have three options that will affect your copy above, you can either: 1) Use a scheduler like Calendly, Acuity, or ScheduleOnce that combine the form and calendar so only one link is required, 2) Use a separate form that redirects to your preferred scheduler or 3) Place the form link and the calendar link in the email and hope they complete the form. We suggest #1 or #2 to maintain a streamlined process.

Producing a Show

Pre-Show Prep

03

Words of Wisdom

Use a task management system to stay organized. By using systems such as Trello, TeamWork, or ClickUp, or Monday - you are able to track when a podcast is airing, what information is missing, store bio information for easy reference, and have a one stop location with interview prep (questions to ask, subjects to avoid, etc) when it is time to go live.

Once the application is received, use your task management system to create an entry for that guest. Systems like TeamWork allow you to auto populate a card once placed on a board so standard tasks are automatically added to it.

Each podcast entry should have a due date of the interview, the guest bio, headshot, preferred questions to be asked (if provided), the introduction you plan to use (if one is not provided - this is normally your standard intro and a brief overview of the guest), interview questions, freebie to be shared, and social media links.

Come prepared to the interview. Take a moment and do your research! Learn about their latest projects, how they are contributing to their niche, and how they got started. Just like any journalist worth their weight, be sure to know who your guest is and what they are going to discuss so you can create a more organic/free flowing/engaging conversation rather than robotically asking provided questions that receive rehearsed answers.

Again, the primary reason for a task management system is to create a trackable podcast schedule to ensure you have everything you need (and can quickly answer inquiries on when certain podcast are airing...because you will be asked!)

PRODUCING A SHOW

PREP BEFORE GOING LIVE

03

WORDS OF WISDOM

Always perform a sound check. By having your guest connect a little early, you are able to test mic levels and determine if there will be any connection issues before starting. Also, sign into your recording device 10 minutes prior to the schedule time. This way if you have any software issues, you have time to troubleshoot without cutting into your interview time.

If your scheduler does not send reminder notices, we recommend creating an automation to send a reminder 24-48 hours prior to the interview time.

Prior to your scheduled interview, sign into your task management system for easy access to your guest data.

Sign into your recording device and do a quick test to make sure everything is working properly before your guest joins. We recommend using **Zoom** as a free option (for podcast under 45 minutes with more than two guests) but some have enjoyed using Squadcast or Riverside. Add in 5-10 minutes of buffer time to do a sound check with your guest and to check connectivity speeds so you don't have buffering or dropping issues during the interview.

Remember to silence all devices, turn off all notifications (anything that may ping, ding, or pop-up and cause a distraction, and if others are at home at the time - let them know you are not to be disturbed (or hang up a sign that says "Recording in session".

Once your guest signs on, test mic levels, listening devices, and playback. Remind them to silence everything on their end as well before getting started.

PODCAST SCHEDULING CHECKLIST

1 CHOOSE RECORDING DEVICE

Decide where interviews will take place - Zoom, Squadcast, Riverside, etc.

2 PICK SCHEDULING PROGRAM

Streamline the scheduling process by having potential guest go directly to a calendar to book a time.

3 PROGRAM FOR SPEAKER FORM

Choose a program to use for your applications. We recommend free options: Jotform and/or Google Form.

4 CREATE A PODCAST SCHEDULE

Choose a task management system that will allow you to stay organized as you schedule more and more guests.

PODCAST GUESTS

Just this a quick place to jot down guests until you set up your task management system.

INVITED	GUEST	ACCEPTED?
☐		YES/NO
☐		YES/NO
☐		YES/NO
☐		YES/NO
☐		YES/NO
☐		YES/NO
☐		YES/NO
☐		YES/NO

Editing a Show

04

Words of Wisdom

If you use royalty free music for your intros and outros, be sure to properly post attributes to avoid copyright issues down the road. You may also want to add a teaser before the audio or a commercial add-on during the podcast to break up podcasts longer than 30 minutes. Transcriptions can be valuable for accessibility and repurposing content; however, if they are being created solely for SEO purposes, the cost may outweigh the benefit depending on your overall content strategy.

If you prefer not to do your own show notes, AI tools can now generate summaries, highlights, and links directly from your audio, saving a significant amount of time. If you'd rather have a human handle it, freelancers are still available on platforms like Fiverr and Upwork to listen to your episode and create summaries for your blog post, social media, and RSS feed.

For simple audio edits, free desktop programs like Audacity are still a solid option. Some AI-assisted editing tools (such as Descript and Emastered.com) can also help speed up basic cleanup. Anything beyond adding an intro, outro, or simple cuts is usually better handled by an audio editor. Upwork has experienced editors who work on a per-episode basis, and we've seen rates low enough that outsourcing is often a better use of time than editing it yourself.

Whether you're editing your own audio or working with a professional editor, Epidemic Sound and BenSound remain solid resources for licensed music suitable for podcast intros and outros.

Promoting a Show

06

Words of Wisdom

Waveform Audio and Video shorts are a perfect way to get your message across to potential listeners as videos have a higher viewing rate on social media. Create a video teaser of your podcast and post it on social media (including TikTok) and YouTube with a link to the podcast.

Once the podcast is posted, notify your guest to give them ample time to promote it to their audience in the manner they see fit.

Using a program such as Descript allows you to create a video or waveform-visual based audio experience to promote on your social media sites. If you took our suggestion above, the individual who created your show notes should have also created social media posts and hashtags to accompany your posts.

For additional exposure, use a truncated version of your show notes and create a blog post on your site as well as a podcast directory. The blog post doesn't need to be more than a few lines along with bio of your guests and the embedded audio player from your podcast platform.

For older listeners who may not utilize social media, create an email blast that goes out the day the podcast is live to increase listeners/exposure.

Overall, your podcast should be posted on your website and all social media platforms. You can even take the audiogram and post it on YouTube to increase your exposure. Don't forget to put a call to action to not only listen to the podcast but to also subscribe!

Publishing a Show

05

Words of Wisdom

Choose a hosting platform that not only creates an RSS feed for you, but simplifies the distribution of your podcast. Also check for storage space. By using your own website versus a third party site such as Libsyn, the audio files saved on your server will eat up your disk space which can cause your site to slow down.

Once the audio files are edited and the show notes are created, it is time to publish the podcast.

First, update the predesigned podcast image(s) in Canva (or your preferred graphic editing software) to show the correct name, image, and title (if applicable and desired) of the guest.

Using the hosting platform of your choice – self-hosted (e.g., Blubrry), free fully hosted option (such as Spotify for Creators) or fully hosted with free/paid options like Buzzsprout, Libsyn, Podbean, Simplecast, or other current hosts – upload your edited audio, add your show notes, add your podcast image, and schedule your podcast. You want to schedule your podcast to post at least 24 hours before you make it live to the public as it could take 24–48 hours for all distribution platforms to pick up your RSS feed and add your podcast. This timeframe is ONLY if your podcast has already been accepted and it is simply adding a new episode to your pre-existing show.

Most of the above programs will provide directions on how to submit your podcast to third-party platforms. If you find you need additional help with this, we can help!

EMAIL TEMPLATE #4
NOTIFY GUEST THAT THEIR PODCAST IS LIVE

Subject: [First Name], Your Podcast Goes Live (Date) *(so if you know you want to have the podcast go live on Fridays - this would be the date shared with them but you would post the audio on Wednesday so it is live on iTunes by Friday)*

Good [Time of Day: Morning/Afternoon/Evening] [First Name],

We are so grateful to have had you on the show. [Your name if you have a podcast manager or I] had an amazing time!

Your podcast will go live bright and early (date) to our audience.

Below is the link to promote and your graphic.

If you need anything else, please let me know.

Audio: link to audio episode
If applicable: Video: link to video episode
Attach cover art for episode

AI Recommendations

- Show Notes:
  - ChatGPT
  - Gemini
- Graphic Design
  - Dalle-E
  - Ideogram
  - Canva
- Audio Editor:
  - Descript
  - Emastered.com
  - Adobe Podcast

The amount of time it takes to delegate the tasks is far more cost effective than doing an entire episode yourself. One episode - from start to finish, can take hours!

Where to Submit Your Podcast

- Apple Podcasts
- Amazon Music (and Audible)
- Spotify
- YouTube Music (Podcasts)
- iHeartRadio
- TuneIn Radio

READY TO GET STARTED?

Workflow Example

We don't know which task management system you will use so it isn't possible to simply "give" you a workflow that you can implement, instead, we have provided an example of one of our podcast setups below to allow you to build your own where you see fit.

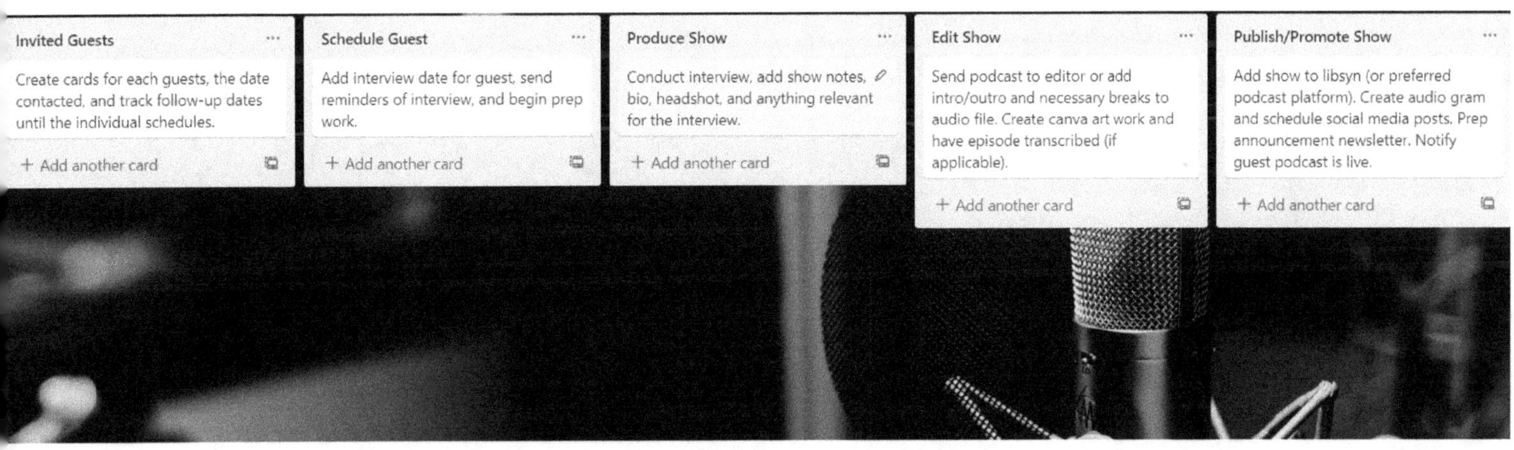

We hope this guide was worth the investment. If you believe we left something out or got something wrong, please let us know so we can update it!

Best wishes on your podcast!!

www.ingramcontent.com/pod-product-compliance
Lightning Source LLC
LaVergne TN
LVHW060046210926
848481LV00013B/3964

* 9 7 9 8 2 9 5 6 3 2 0 7 5 *